First published 2000 by Walker Books Ltd
87 Vauxhall Walk, London SE11 5HJ

2 4 6 8 10 9 7 5 3 1

Series concept and design by Louise Jackson

Words by Paul Harrison and Louise Jackson

Wildlife consultant: Martin Jenkins

This book has been typeset in Lemonade.

Printed in Singapore

British Library Cataloguing in Publication Data
A catalogue record for this book is available
from the British Library.

ISBN 0-7445-6253-8

COLOURS

illustrated by
Sue Hendra

WALKER BOOKS
AND SUBSIDIARIES
LONDON • BOSTON • SYDNEY

black

pink

No...but I've got **white** feathers on my tummy. My feathers are thick and keep me warm in my icy home.

black

grey

green

green

orange

red

black

orange

grey

white

yellow

grey

orange

yen

...t I've got
...tail. I use
...o help me
...ance.

blue

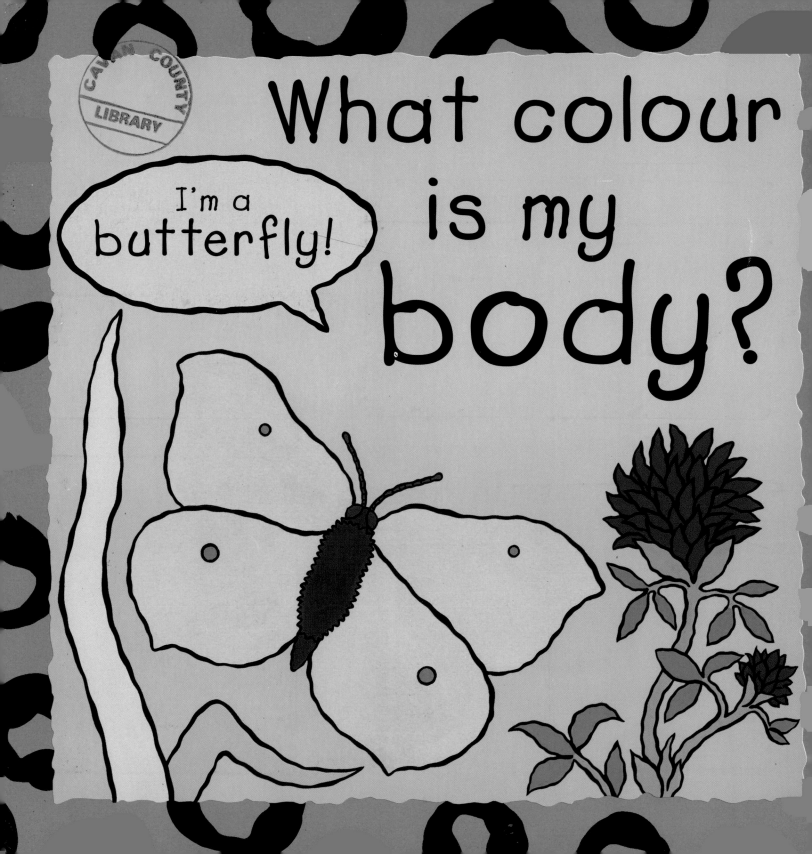

yellow

brown

No...but I've got **red** feelers on top of my head. I use my feelers to smell with.

Can you match the colours to the animals?

orange
claws

green
wings

black
nose

brown
body

grey
fur

red
eyes

pink
feet